Gather the Night

Mary Burritt Christiansen Poetry Series

Mary Burritt Christiansen Poetry Series
Hilda Raz, Series Editor

The Mary Burritt Christiansen Poetry Series publishes two to four books a year that engage and give voice to the realities of living, working, and experiencing the West and the Border as places and as metaphors. The purpose of the series is to expand access to, and the audience for, quality poetry, both single volumes and anthologies, that can be used for general reading as well as in classrooms.

Also available in the Mary Burritt Christiansen Poetry Series:

The Handyman's Guide to End Times: Poems by Juan J. Morales
Rain Scald: Poems by Tacey M. Atsitty
A Song of Dismantling: Poems by Fernando Pérez
Critical Assembly: Poems of the Manhattan Project by John Canaday
Ground, Wind, This Body: Poems by Tina Carlson
MEAN/TIME: Poems by Grace Bauer
América invertida: An Anthology of Emerging Uruguayan Poets
    edited by Jesse Lee Kercheval
Untrussed: Poems by Christine Stewart-Nuñez
The Woman Who Married a Bear: Poems by Tiffany Midge
Family Resemblances: Poems by Carrie Shipers

For additional titles in the Mary Burritt Christiansen Poetry Series, please visit unmpress.com.

Gather the Night

POEMS

Katherine DiBella Seluja

UNIVERSITY OF NEW MEXICO PRESS • ALBUQUERQUE

Library of Congress Cataloging-in-Publication Data
Names: Seluja, Katherine DiBella, 1959– author.
Title: Gather the night: poems / Katherine DiBella Seluja.
Description: Albuquerque: University of New Mexico Press, 2018. | Includes
   bibliographical references. |
Identifiers: LCCN 2017060911 (print) | LCCN 2018003859 (e-book) |
   ISBN 9780826359896 (e-book) | ISBN 9780826359889 (pbk.: alk. paper)
Classification: LCC PS3619.E4684 (e-book) | LCC PS3619.E4684 A6 2018 (print) |
   DDC 811/.6—dc23
LC record available at https://lccn.loc.gov/2017060911

Cover photograph: *There Is You* by Gustavo Angel Seluja, 2011

for Lou

A schizophrenic is no longer schizophrenic . . .

when he feels understood by someone else.

—Carl G. Jung

Contents

Sing to Me

Stars Speak

TIME TRAVEL

Stunning truly stunning all that purple red purpled blew up all over the sky but Einstein was up late again on the roof working on that box it's gonna' take time travel to the whole next level something like wax and ice cold purple that stings if you get too close it never talks out loud because you know what happens if you whisper don't you the stars watching every night but Einstein doesn't care he just keeps on burning and splashing new thoughts and words that glide and schloom I told him when he's in the tub he should turn the radio off the water always screams way too loud

Storm Hymn

One thin crack in the plastic sign
on the locked ward door

winds its way through
Authorized Personnel Only

like a branch of the Hackensack River
where we used to play.

Dried mud thick on our shoes
split in so many places,

our mother's face when she said,

We just admitted your brother;
he told us his crystals were melting.

Waiting for the orderly to turn his key

I turn back to our winter childhood refuge
under the cellar stairs.

We were base camp
guardians of snow

charted drift and temperature
graphed hope for Sunday night storms.

Now gray clouds
and Thorazine doses increase,

he wanders the blizzard alone
no guide rope tied to the door,

unique as each stellar dendrite
no two of him alike.

Kata

1

Each week he binds his waist, white or yellow sash
heads out to lunge and jab.

I long to pull on that robe, throw the boys to the mat.

2

His size twelve foot above my head, the draft it makes as it passes.

At fifteen, my brother
six-foot-one

used me as punching bag.
He practiced the deliberate kicks called karate.

3

He wants me to know *defend*, wants me to be prepared.
He speaks center of gravity, Adam's apple.

Clean whack to the larynx buys time
sharp heel to the instep an opportunity.

The day I found him frozen in the kitchen
all his instruction fell cold to the floor.

Chiquita

Lou would meet us there.
He'd ride my green Stingray, knees thumping handlebars.

Reynaldo and I would walk.

Reynaldo was the renter from across the street and always called me
    chiquita.
I'd laugh and wonder why he thought I was a banana.

Reynaldo took my hand and led me down the block,
away from squares of front yard grass, away from straight front
    walk.

We headed down the hill toward the tracks.
Lou would come flying down that hill any minute, his six-foot frame
    folded

into a blur of Schwinn. We came to the park near the tracks and the
tunnel that passed underneath, scene of many childhood dares.

We used to challenge our cousins to race that dank stretch on only
    one breath
avoiding the dark spots on the tunnel floor.

Reynaldo led me down the stairs. Halfway down he stopped and
    turned around,
stepped backward down two more steps.

His face level with mine, I saw the pimples on his nose.
He leaned in close,

asked me how I liked the feel of his tongue.

Adirondack Green

You would have to be Adirondack green mountains

to know why the brother who climbed through dark windows
was sent there, farm school in the hills.

You would have to be A-frame construction and fifteen-foot beams,
hold the weight of February, walk the last mile in.

You would have to be backseat quiet on that twelve-hour ride
past Albany gray granite, winding Glens Falls.

You would have to be the tacit bull led through barnyard gate,
shot with nervous fingers and a .22.

You would have to be the broken trellis, the slate that fell from the
roof, the slit in the seam of the jeans.

Local Grown

Long before the first twenty-four-hour Pathmark lit up Cedar Lane

There was Scottie, the grocer. His smile crisp as the Granny Smiths brought over from Hartley's Farm in Essex County. He called my mother by name. Handpicked the best nectarines fresh off the truck from Dover. Only the sweetest thin-skinned peaches, setting aside those with the dark-brown bruise.

Long before we spent our summer evenings roaming the air-conditioned aisles

There was Mr. Jimmie, the butcher. Pork loin straight off the stockyard car from Newark. Top sirloin hand-fed through the grinder. His white apron splotched bright red. A choice cut for our family, excess fat hand-trimmed.

Long before fluorescent light illuminated all of our choices

There was Mrs. Gratzel, the baker's wife. Her apron pulled tight as she reached over hot cross buns, hamantaschen, and soda bread. Always a cookie or two slipped around the glass case for the children. And Mr. Gratzel at the ovens in the back, flour sifting softly from his fingers.

Neighborhood Of

Staying at a friend's apartment in the city, I walk out without noticing the address. I stroll the city streets in search of city treasures and then, realizing the time and needing to get to the lecture I am expected to attend, I return and circle round to discover I am close-but-no-cigar in the right neighborhood. I circle the alleys, hunt the avenues, lope down side streets numbered odd then even with directional arrows going one way and then another, and I am no way in charge of this adventure—I am lost. I am at the mercy of the city streets: wide and full and cramped and hollow. Hours of circling, closer at times and further at others to realize I am alone and in need of help, someone to lend a hand and if only I had written down the address, paid attention to the cross street, had a phone; when finally it occurs to me to ask a man chatting with a group of friends on a park bench. I describe the apartment setting and I know it's somewhere near Twelfth Street but I'm not exactly sure and of course he knows the area and of course he can give me a ride as my knee that has been troubling since the day I decided to paint the entire bathroom on my own has been acting up again, all this ambling and strolling and running and walking has definitely flared the ligament and isn't it wonderful when we remember to write the little things down?

She Wore Opals at Her Neck

He fell in love with the mahogany curve
her hip and polish

the rosewood waist
and the way her neck fit to his palm.

Bella he called her for the ancient orchard of her birth.

He carried her everywhere
coated in beeswax and chamois.

Ninina he called her for the tuner who had laid down her frets.

At night he saw her inlaid eyes
floating in the dark before him.

She would hum while he slept
melodies of twist and branch.

Bella he called her for the ancient orchard
and the apprentice's hand that carved her.

Carina he called her for the notes he pulled from her strings.

Three Kites

All in one day, three kites.
Two bombarding the air above the park,
twins of twist and dive above swings
and baseball diamonds,
above our streets of daily blue.

And later, another park
filled with roses and a boy unwinding
his triangle of red and blue.
Others stop to watch him navigate the evening
light deepening into diamonds.

A kite is where a soul might park,
that long thread that spans the evening,
alternating lax or taut,
connects the body like long-stemmed roses
bred over generations for fewer thorns
but more blue fragrance.

Grasp

The fingers of my brother's hands are callused.

He stretches one hand far across steel strings.
Near the Bay of Fundy, fishermen repair their nets.

Brother, why do you grasp the mandolin neck tighter than the
    bottle?
Why, Sister, this bottle still is made of glass.

Self-Inflicted

After the blast he staggered
shattered foot dragged half a mile

meant only to clean the barrel
wooden stock against truck seat.

He had been alone
the truck was cold and still

her photo torn or crumpled
certain the lock was on.

All the while he muttered
what she would have said:

There you go again
selfish with your things

careless with all the weight of wonder.

You Left the Candle All Night

after Rilke, Evening

Slowly the evening turns to dark
coyotes peer in from the edge
you have lit a candle
you have held the beads
you have turned your bed to the East
and yet
the shaking comes
the trembling jaw.

You are alone in the midst of many
your life afraid and huge and ripening
smelling of burnt milk
and fish flesh.

For the fifth time you have checked the lock
not quite so dark as the house sunk in silence
or the smoke that seeps from the sage.

When you can breathe again
you search for the evening star

to still the shaking
unwind the knot
a tonic for the deepest tremor
the smooth stone that hangs from your neck.

Ice Candle Recipe

Prepare the container of your choice
old milk cartons work best.

Heat wax over low flame.
Add crushed ice to container.

He taught himself the mandolin.
A teacher had shown him a few chords.

At nineteen, his first psychotic break.
It was something that ran in the family.

As molten surrounds frozen
a labyrinth of caves is left behind.

Maybe because it was spring, maybe the E string was tight
but the sheen in his eye made me want to white out my tongue.

I waited several days before telling our parents
Lou had turned into wax.

Dipping the Dead

It was a high school job
second shift, tropical fish warehouse

walking the scale-strewn aisles
bubbling tanks stacked three high

moisture and fluorescent light
and the chore that no one wanted

removal of each carcass
bloated midnight skin

some missing eye or fin
scoop and thud of net on plastic tub

feral cats whining at the door.

Blue Dye on Eggshell

The rule is nature will stain you
don't try to color it back.

Onion skins boiled, acorns brewed
berry and beet crushed on stone

each will produce its own texture
steeping will heighten the hue.

Steaming liquid in porcelain bowls
put aside hard-boiled white

these are the scenes you will tint:

> your father weaving green Sunday cross of palm
> your brother shrinking in gray sheets

> a field at dawn filled with sudden violets.

Dredge and slurry each surface.

See how the shade will deepen, the longer you hold it beneath.

For Webster's Next Edition

schizoid: walking on stilts in the ocean

manic: ladder-back woodpecker in the lumber aisle

frenetic: thousands of blue-legged crabs spinning on one leg

paranoid: two breaths for every room

incessant: why it wasn't me

insane: you

FREE CONCERT

That girl again the one with the hair that always sings like you can't hear fifty decibels too loud walking in circles with pink slippers and carrying her little wand in my room last night chanting spells that only Einstein could understand what was she saying about alfalfa and asparagus and growing her own in the backyard was I at Woodstock and did I hear Paul Simon at the free concert in Central Park the nurses think she's tame but I would watch out for that one twirling in those little pink shoes

Of Calamine and Honey

Make a list
of all that is broken.

Mandolin strings
his cherry-tree face

and all that is amniotic.

Children's feet scuffle
over cracks in the sidewalk

wide enough
for three small pebbles

and nests of wasp.

You can't go on that way,
only thorns to catch your fall

and his words
buzzing at your ankles

searching for the tender spot.

Admission

Mason jars, splashes of light, and not enough room for his legs, he ran up to the roof thinking about Einstein and how color theory would look after he died. The edge of the roof was singing and the space beyond so incredibly soft. Soft as the blanket of cornfields he had seen at his uncle's farm in Ohio. Did he have an uncle in Ohio? The space beyond the roof was calling his name, maybe just dip his toes, stir the air surrounding the gutters. The birds all seem to understand how to move softly through that space, so softly.

The Psychiatrist Said

It's in the bloodlines.

We can trace the illness back three to four hundred years.
Wax eyes   frozen face   poverty of speech.

And Lou's dreaming of a '68 Mustang
like the one our parents bought him

the winter before he stole the stereo
before the mandolin was pawned.

Hood vent   square cut   spokes on the wheel.

The shrink jumps in the car
complaining about backseat drivers

and tells Lou to take a left at the light.

It's all a matter of proteins.
We'll have it cracked in three to four years.

And Lou goes along for the ride
searching the rearview mirror, alternating his speed.

Rupture so much closer than it seems.

Stigmata

Ride down the turnpike sunset stigmata searching an exit we never knew sent on a mission of wax and ice by parents who missed the signs whose ears were too full or turned off instead of broken on a ride no one wanted in a broken down car searching the sign on the locked ward door stigmata of turn signal sun going down into wax on the floor the day his candle burned down he never winced he never cried he was the one that could sing with a cool as ice voice the girls all wanted the brother with a beard at fifteen who sounded like Graham Nash and played like Jimmie and it looked like he would go the same way filled with wax and blood ice in his mouth in his ears in his head and no room left for sanity or anything close to that exit.

Locked Ward

Thirty-four years before
he was a patient at Greystone

our mother was a student nurse there
plaiting a patient's long gray hair.

The woman grabbed the braid
and wrapped it tight around our mother's neck.

She also slipped the shiny scissors
from our mother's starched white pocket.

Long before he was there.

When Your Son Is Diagnosed in the 1960s

It's a cord that wraps itself around a cord
that carries electricity and blood.

They say it might work, they say it might not
just a little buzz and sting.

They say don't worry, go home and cook dinner, don't worry
we know it's all your fault.

His psychosis is tied to your mothering
and it's time to cut the cord, be careful of the sting.

He'll be just like the day you brought him home
wrapped in a blue blanket drooling.

So what if you have to teach him how
to hold a spoon, the difference between yellow and burn.

Never mind his rubber-soled shoes,
he won't be needing them yet.

Schizophrenia

Snakes have slid from Paul's guitar
vibrating in the key of G.

My brother tries for the harmony
only single grunts escape.

His mouth is crammed with eighth notes
sliding down his throat.

His elbow is a pulley
his hand an iron claw.

And then he sees her

the girl in the hospital dayroom
grasping and plucking the air

quarter notes
dripping down her arm.

How to Walk on Water

A crowd of blind believers is useful.

Distract them
with fresh loaves and wine.

Think mallard rather than cattail,
oak leaf lighter than autumn.

Let the ripples spread out from your toes.
Let murmur sound like miracle.

Spinning with Thorazine

> Charge the carder by taking it in your left hand
> with your right hand lay staples of wool across the metal pins
> distribute the wool evenly over the entire card
> until teeth are barely showing through
>
> —*The Joy of Hand Spinning*

Now he's a pillow
or a block of ice

wrapped in cotton gauze
eyes a matted quilt

lashes pulled mid-stitch.

Soft thud of cotton slippers
gather lint from the floor.

Young woman in the dayroom corner
pulls at wisps of air

what hospice nurses call reaching for the angels.

Dayroom Girl

I bet he could make it sing real good. He carried that thing everywhere. Never set it down, never let anybody hold it even for a glance, probably slept with it for all I know. Now where is it? What's he done with that pint-sized guitar? I heard smashing and crying from his end of the hall. Kept everybody awake until the night nurse finally put a stop to it. Haven't heard him now in days. Somebody said they got him in the white room, tied up real tight, no visitors, no mail, no momma singing to him in between the bars and for sure no little guitar swooning or swaying its way on back into his life. What's that boy gonna' do now without his stringy little sweetheart?

Canyon Towhee

His extremities pinned
in four-point restraints

desperate pull and flap
must be something like final

moments of the canyon towhee
I found floating in red cooler.

Wings splayed, legs stiff, claws stretched, reaching.

A rain that fell too hard
a cooler lid left open.

Frantic flapping led to stillness.

September moon
slung low

soft hiss
of breath through beak.

Jorge Jumped Three Times

from the roof and had such crappy luck he survived all three and Bob the vet only nods and yelps all day. Dickie is wound so tight you could motor the whole New Jersey turnpike off of him. He walks in circles until they call for therapy and then that shaggy art lady comes with the cart filled with all the second-grade coloring stuff, like crayons and Easter baskets but no scissors or glue for sure, no scissors or glue. And then there's Mandy with her sweet little running down the beach bare-foot body. She tried Valium and Tylenol and a fifth of her father's gin and that still didn't take her down. But they brought her in on a stretcher all right. Ralph the janitor told me he had to clean up the mess after they pumped her stomach. Now she sits there humming that sad song, Horse with No Name or Midnight Cowboy. The doc comes every Tuesday. He's letting his hair go a little longer, thinks that'll be enough to get us to open up and share and all the while I'm saving up my phone time to call my sister to see if she can come get me outta' here. My parents visit when they can but Dad is a lump of wax and Mom is always talking lasagna or spaghetti and then she starts crying and I feel like my skin is jumping off my back. The next thing you know I'm smashing the wall and the guys in white are tying me down. I wish they would let me the heck out, I could crawl through the air vent, slide down the drainpipe, sneak into that supply truck, and ride on up Route 80 anywhere far from here.

Spread Wide Your Arms That Might Be Wings

Re-sheath those blades that might be shoulders

inhale your heart
let nothing weigh you there

beneath the sternum
count the pulse of the day.

Let each one come bidden or not, seen or unseen.

Drop the shield,
peel the layers built from years

of heartbreak and broken bone,
your body will let you down.

Just when you were so sure you were immortal

so sure
all the little gods would invite you in

their broad planked tree house, the rope ladder released

bottles of mead
and dulce de leche on the table, there

at least a few feet from the ground
you see yourself, finally

feasting with the gods.

Lines Found on the Dayroom Floor

after Sarah Messer

Jammed into the nurse's pocket
to hold something close to nothing

Spoken as an invocation
your life floats in a wine bottle

Line to be dropped with no anchor
how many coins for a packet of rice

Tied in a knot on his finger
will she keep me warm

Cast into the ocean
only the cork to save you

Furled from the top of the rigging
this your shining hour

Line from the midnight sergeant
fourth floor casement window

Repeated in the village of memory
only a courtyard view

Banner left at the summit
opportunity or restraint

Burnt with saffron and turmeric
air your greatest achievement

Offering in ceramic bowl
bare toes on oak windowsill

Love Letter from the Ninth Floor

You didn't see me. I was high above you, on the ninth floor, yeah the locked ward.

Crazytown.

But I saw you. Walking across the parking lot. Heading toward that blue Miata with the top down.

You stopped by the side of the car rummaging for your keys. I saw your hair blowing and I could smell the strawberry conditioner you used this morning.

What were you doing here? Who did you come to visit?

Your mother recovering from hip surgery, your father after a stroke, a boyfriend who broke his leg falling from a ladder, I hope he'll be laid up for a while.

Or maybe you think that boyfriend gave you a nasty disease, or you've been feeling kind of down lately and need some medication, maybe you had to get a blood test done, can't imagine anyone breaking through that pearly skin of yours, not even the tiniest little poke.

If you had turned slightly, glanced up at the window, I know you would've seen me.

I was sending you the sign, now, now look up here, at a plane, a cloud moving over the sun, a flutter at the edge of your view.

What I wouldn't give for you to visit me. What I wouldn't trade for a ride with you in that little blue car cruising the highway, stopping by the lake, letting the day swirl by.

SING TO ME

The soap went down the drain into the mud the rats the people living there really living and breathing in the drains all over the city I never knew there were so many that's where they go like the girl with the hair at the hospital she's been in that drain before she has that look that I can fit my body through these little holes that open up at night look big enough for the whole floor to drop right through that's why wood is so precious now wood and gold hammering on the roof Einstein asked me to bring up more nails but who knows what nails sound like these days when I got up there he was swinging his feet back and forth back forth I could see it wasn't really that far I could sweep my fingers right through the stars and that's when I knew

Discharge

He was released at five o'clock. Shoes in plastic bag. Empty wallet.
Car keys.
But where had he left the car?

He had no memory of his arrival.
It had been cold, he knew that, because he recalled hours of shaking.
Now it seemed spring was breaking through every crack and he had
to be careful not to slip right through. So many glorious fractures.
So much space. Breathing.

There was the space between the tulip stamens, the space between
the legs of the aphids crawling on the iris, the space between the cell
walls of every living thing.
What had the doctor said?
Don't be surprised if you fall back into one of the many black holes in
your life.

He was pacing the parking lot waiting for a sign from his car and
trying not to notice that the streets beyond the hospital were
opening and closing in rhythm with his lungs.
His hands were sweating around the keys and the empty wallet in
his back pocket was boring a hole into his body.

He considered walking back inside.
He would stay a little longer.
He would unscrew all the light bulbs to stop their chattering
and get right back into that metal-frame bed.
Maybe then he could sew the lines together.
Maybe the fractures would finally stop calling.

The doc said he was ready.

But what if he was only one more half-built vehicle in the long
factory line of incomplete humans? What if the guy who was
supposed to wire up his neurons had taken an extra long lunch
break and the woman who solders the emotional grid called in sick

because her daughter had been vomiting all night? What if his body had passed right through the line without ever being inspected by quality control?

By now he had circled the parking lot three times and had not seen one vehicle that looked like anything he had ever driven.

He stuffed the keys into his pocket and headed toward the bus stop, jumping cleanly over the crevasse as it opened in front of the hospital gate.

If Bacchus Had Left the Party Early

If he had lost his fennel staff

if he had been born of one mother instead of two

if he had never warmed to the taste of grapes

or fermentation were reversed.

Would he have refused the screaming thirst

if the acetyl group didn't bind so quickly

if our DNA had been exchanged

would I have been the one standing outside the Circle K

trading tricks for a bottle of gin?

He Who Gathers the Night

Soft coal blue flame
land with no rain.

Nest cracked or broken
a place he won't call home.

Smoke from the bed of the fire
embers glow at his feet.

Juniper cane his walking stick
cholla thorn his needle.

He wanders high desert alone.
He who wrangles the storm wailing in his ears.

He who gathers the night
his rope thrown among stars.

Mojave Midnight

1

glazing slivers of stars
feet in the sand poppies closed tight
cholla ropes coyote bones cans
thrown from a passing car window
rum and coke lime floating

2

lights strung out at oasis
palm fronds under my feet
guests keep their eyes on horizon
is it owl or vulture above?

3

black lace and cards on a table
an ace pulled from the sand
dust in all of my creases
bottle of rum at my feet

4

collecting on all of my losses
star shards fall from the sky
I brought my voice to a whisper
only the pulse in my groin

5

full of zodiac pining
to long for a change in sign
alone in the house of my homeland
a twin a scale and a ram
flames shoot from my fingers
chanting and waiting for dawn

Travel Log

The Moon

He bounced along for miles over the silver dust.

Floating above the surface,
at times landing hard against rock.

Stones flew hundreds of meters with the barest turn of the wrist.

At some point he missed Buddy Holly,
at some point Kentucky Fried Chicken.

On a day that seemed like Sunday he paused to consider the earth,
cloud shrouded.

High Desert

The prickly pear was browning,
How many for a meal?

He spent hours in the shade
and then trudged the arroyo at sundown.

At night he picked cholla needles from his soles.

Once before dawn a coyote grazed his arm.
He spoke to tarantulas whenever possible but rarely sang to
grasshoppers.

It was months before he discovered his well was broken.

La Playa

Sand under his toenails, in the lining of his shoes.

At some point, he decided to plant poppies.
Red preferable to white and pea rock was always tempting.

As a boy he could never resist any sea gift washed to the shore.
Filled buckets lined the porch by the time they were packing the car.

And our mother, always urging him to choose.

Dragon

on your shoulder

tail nonstop twitching

fire down your gullet all night

iridescent scales float in your head

impossible to consider anything but squelching the fire

hard to focus when the CVS store manager gives you a try

stocking shelves, not too demanding

but so much Cover Girl so much Oil of Olay

so many Crest whitening cotton anklets plastic headbands

tiny teeth run along the edge

chew down any thought of sober

how heavy that dragon

how sharp the teeth that finally bled you dry.

Delirium Tremens

Let the glass sweat and bleed
let the foam run dry.

Walk away from the drink
and let the shaking begin.

Turn to the buzzing in your head
flies at an oozing wound

canyons scream at your feet.
Hold tight to that wad of sheets heaving

at the edge of the bed.
Your bed is a boat and it's swaying,

swinging to a reggae beat
and the ants just won't stop crawling

treading down your arm,
a track for the beetles to follow.

Last night you must have killed twenty

snapping crack of blue-green carapace
beneath your trembling feet.

Arguing with Cirrhosis

You should be glad it never happened.
No drunken sperm of yours could ever have found her lopsided egg.

Yes, she was your childhood sweetheart and yes, her family moved
to the block just as June was beginning to thrum, her younger sister
running hide-and-seek with the fireflies and rugged limbs of oak.

But your liver enzymes are soaring now, higher than the tree in their
side yard.

If she had had your baby, would its skin have gone as yellow as the
edges of your eyes are now? Would it have screamed at night, its
belly sucking in all the air in the room? Just as your belly is filling
now with fluid squeezing backward out of the wrinkled straw that
was your portal vein.

But we were picturing babies.

And you were telling me how you still see chestnut eyes gleaming in
the dark and feel fingers clutching at your chest as you stroke your
protruding abdomen and marvel how after all these years and so
many sloe gin fizzes, a man like you could somehow, finally, gestate.

Telephone, 4 a.m.

Wrapped in muslin night

scream of ringing phone,
his stumbling voice gagging,

Emergency room, again.

And you think,

What if there were a box to keep him in
somewhere to store him away

to bring out with rainy weather.
Then you'd have time to listen, unravel every line.

You'd be awake already

sipping vanilla mint tea
your favorite blue-glazed mug.

The one with the crack that resembles
the shining scar on his forehead.

How sharp that metal gutter
the night he flew from the roof.

Notes to the Evening Nurse

It's in the fold
and crease

accordion pleat
dull-white sheet.

Remember to roll him toward you,
fanfold the length of his spine.

At the dark moist line
between bed and back

there is the site of your labor.

Lean in and know it deep.
Never mind

four more are waiting,
ignore the clock on the wall.

Tell him the month of your birthday,
secret of your grandmother's sauce.

Sing him a song from Old Broadway,
even if you don't know the tune

even if you've never believed

hearing is the last sense to go—
lean in and sing to that being

lying in white at the door.

STARS SPEAK

A special sign between us

the girl in the drain

strings like worms
stars buzz with the rain

when I'm cold or hungry

the stars speak and I know a gift is coming
a blanket or shoes or not getting slammed in the face

or a really good spot in the tunnel
so the mandolin can get some rest

The History of Healing

It began as a huddle of knowers, passed through oral tradition,
those who could "heal" and those who at least attempted.

There were the leeches, yes, and that unfortunate period of
bloodletting, but there was also foxglove and penicillium.

It began as a group, those who knew and those who were called.

Small hands and a good memory were needed, a willingness to go
with less sleep, the ability to travel quickly or keep a good beast.

Certainly a stomach for blood, bile, afterbirth.
It passed through oral tradition.

Back then it was often women and often men.
It was children sent from a distance to learn.

Some slept on the floor near the fire,
some slumped in a chair, a few slept on their feet.

Always the skill of observation and the ability to read the small signs,
the quickening of pulse, mottling of skin, reddening at the edge
of the wound.

They didn't need much nourishment and they learned to share the
crust: less weight meant faster travel through the night.

To Reduce the Swelling

Drop the shovel
bury the can filled with ashes

to relieve the bruising
make ice, apply anything attached to a bone

a dislocation

pain eventually lessens
by the time the bruises yellow

you will either be well or be numb.

Sticks and goat heads buried in sand
we suffer

ghost hair, pumpkin seeds, and the vine that creeps.

There between the floor-boards,
mouse droppings and egret feathers.

To decrease the swelling
borrow your neighbor's ice-cream maker, slow churn
and a recognition of form.

Is it mineral or vegetable that creaks in the hallway at night
on your way to the freezer for a fresh bag of ice?

The seeping bruise, the turn and sway

something to place on the molar,
to chew the other side

the sting that wakes you, not pain
but the dull thud of the root that comes first.

News of a Brother's Death

Don't kid yourself,
it's nothing like a movie.

No subtitles to clarify meaning,
no forewarning minor key
the police found him
in his apartment
no change of lens to soften
the edges of scene.

Only my clinic office,
a patient's nebulizer hum
nurses shouting vitals from another room.

Rude light from cubicle window
glare of black-corded phone

and that sudden break in the reel
right after I hear the caller say

dead on the floor.

Blue Vase

empty
translucent container

to hold your only duty
how many bouquets did you miss

gaze through blue glass
thorns come into view

long-stemmed wonder
garland of barren questions

what of the funneled calla
the wilting lily

baby's breath
torn and frayed

still your tangled roots
mildew in gray water

rest now
floating brown-leaf posy

Why Our Mother Hated Lilies

Easter lilies, tall and leaning.

Waxy trumpet flower,
green stamens that protrude.

Explore the cup of blossom
standing at attention.

And the smell.

What used to seem so spring,
so Easter basket, so third day he rose again

now is detestable.

Why our mother hated lilies and I never knew.

Until our sister gone, parents gone and now you
dead on the floor.

Aluminum foil wraps the pot, the container must be contained
like Victorian piano legs, the burka, closed casket.

We left your casket open and I am staring at your face
and inhaling the stink of lilies.

Weight of Hyacinth

Two point two pounds
of infant born too soon

little mole born of the family Talpidae.
Gelatinous skin eyes fused

a weight that fits in my hand
legs no thicker than tulip stems.

No matter she is barely breathing,
no matter the cyanotic blue

or the mewing that slides from her throat.
Place the gelatinous bulb on the scale

and decide if it's a weight that matters.
Will the tiny breathing machine be equal

to six months of care hand cut down to size
or will the mole be returned to the earth

for further gestation of loam
months of root and tuber?

Starburst nose scraping tongue
a newborn delivered from earth

progeny of Persephone
babygod in a wheelbarrow

pushed through paper white tangles
erupted from furrow and straw.

For the Mother Who Fed Her Children Grass: A Blessing

May you never cook leaves and salt
and offer it to hungry children

yerba and oil stand alone on the shelf
never cook leaves and salt.

May you never carry your baby
down Ramón Anador begging for milk or rice

knocking at thresholds trembling,
never carry your baby down.

May you never long for two stomachs
one to ruminate cud,

one a chamber for holding
both contract when empty.

May you never forage the yard
dried *butia* wrinkled and brown

pounding to break down the fiber
never sever the stem.

May you never consider the price
weighing each bony piece

soaking to soften the veins
never cook leaves and salt.

The Empty Peace of Lung

That last full breath
slides gently from the chest.

Peace, that place
that fills with rushing water.

When every bone is laid to rest
every inhalation done,

carve the character for sorrow.

Sparrow nest in his mouth,
Soñar no cuesta nada, said my mother.

Peace, you cheated me
still no footstone for his grave.

A certain rashing quiet on the surface of the skin,
this is the last time I will say it:

There are bones that bend not break,
there are breaths I will not take.

No me hace nada, said my dead brother.

You Will Find It in the Stillness

You will christen him with saline
wash the noise and tape away

acetone ghosting from the room.

You will wrap his tiny form
in the sheet they call morgue pack.

Only pale-white morning moons remain.

When the ventilator's incessant
waves of breathing come to rest,

when persistent pulsing
monitor is done,

when the shining beads of moisture
inside his breathing tube are gone,

pale-white morning moons remain.

It is then that you will feel
the ancient mantle on your chest

drop like sodden wool
yet light as infant's breath,

it is then that you will bow
your head and mumble ragged prayer

silent awkward praise.

Do Our Ancestors Listen When Called

Or are they busy translating prayers and nebulae, granting blessings
and galaxies, directing newborns and photons into the descending
line?

We can understand time bending in space, our ancestors figured it
out, you need to be good at lifting your feet from the ground.

Take the last pulsar out, be late for the eclipse, run shoeless
over magnetic fields, kiss the wild boar's snout.

My heart is occupied with the ones I've lost, each with its own
celestial sphere, their pulse echoes the meridian.

I keep rearranging you like a favorite satellite, dragging you
into good orbit, your solar panels deployed to the stars.

Here Among the Ruins

> I don't know how to walk here among the ruins
> —Gregorio

Among the pot shards and pelvic bones,
deep within a cave

in Cantabria prehistoric remains are found.

I don't know how to breathe among the dust and vinegar
the broken shrines.

Reflection of my dead brother
in the eyes of a nephew who tells me he's addicted to life.

No hope no horsehair
nothing to wipe the dog's paws.

I don't know how to pause among the ashes
the piñon burnt to a stub.

I can't swim here among the herons,
all their fine feathers weighing me down.

I don't know how to speak the unspoken
dropped lines cover the floor

words already enunciated
my mouth heavy with rocks and ice.

If What We Have is Incomplete

1

If the ink runs dry.

If the fair-skinned woman is covered

in swans and compasses.

If the grinding pull of skin is renamed: *human attempting divinity.*

Is this the magnetic draw to leave our mark?

If what we have is incomplete—

nest with a stillborn chick,

then egg, abandoned.

2

Another time I would have called you,

would have pulled the nest from the tree.

Another time,

a nest filled with paper fortunes.

Another, an artificial tree.

3

I can't stop buying trees,

planting them in your name.

4

Every tequila shot, every air guitar,

every crumpled dollar bill offered

through half-open car window,

all done in your honor.

Undeniably Human

1

It was something around the eyes or the lobe of the ear.

The way hair was flipped over a shoulder, an elbow stroked.

More than the curve of fingernail,

the undone button,

a certain lisp.

2

Was it a smudge of mascara or a wrinkle near the lid?

The way the room was approached and then entered,

pause on the bottom step?

And if she hadn't taken the stairs, had been transported in a box of steel

one level to the next—

3

The lilacs are brilliant and sickening.

I close every window in the house.

Behind pulled shades, do our neighbors plan their futures or their demise?

A girl throws a rock for hopscotch, chalked boxes numbered one to nine.

Enough room for one foot only in the half-moon rest stop.

If You Need a Wall

Gather moon gray
fieldstones black

river rock beetles,
level your ground

extract every weed.
Divining rod in hand

consider its height.

Let the children etch
curlicue *y*'s and *g*'s.

Your neighbor will lean
there careless

robin might drop a twig.
Wild lily and gourd will curl

at its base mix mortar
water from your father's well

or your grandmother's almanac.
Summer may wrap it in heat

ice will brittle each crevice.
There's room for crayon drawings,

his wide-ruled love note,
Saint Anne's birthday card.

It will contain your life,
leave it open

for chocolate-brown quail,
mud to frost each layer

or blue pebbles picked from the shore.
You'll need a stout trowel

work swiftly,
mortar sets faster than grief.

The Function of Ghosts

1
The ghost, it seemed, had promised
to watch over us months after its body
was placed in the ground.

Often I'd wake and sense it
quiet but sure as the mantel clock,
the dog's sigh.

I said nothing
of these visitations
to my family.

2
Translucent being

you inhale my sleeping
breath: cat in the newborn's crib.

3
Transporter
of unstated desire

still as porcelain figures
hand carried from a distant country.

A couple seated side by side
on horse-drawn cart.

The cart itself holds citrus candy,
paper wrapped.

This, the sweetness.

Three Stones

On my way to visit my brother's grave
I pass another's
and see three stones resting
on the marker of Nathan Solomon, devoted son.

Three small fragments of earth positioned
to remind us of your connection loyal father
now so intimate with the ground.
A symbol that hums to those who may come after—
One has come before you.

Someone stood here, as I do now
peered into infinity and placed a stone as if to say:
All we know comes down to this encrypted
bit of earth, this small yet solid nugget
that one can hold, this is where the struggle ends.

Wanderlust

in the weft of that rich manifold
—Rilke, *Prayer*

Find me
in the weave of my brother's shirt,
in the tread of mud on the floor.

Pull me from the sand.

Let the sinking sun
unwind across the sea.

A fisherman gathers his work of the day,
folding wet squares of net.

Shall my face not forever stand out

a mermaid longing for rescue,
a dinghy with no oar?

And where is the wandering beggar?

His pack tied to my cane,
we let loose the dog from the yard.

Luminescent

Certainly not in the cemetery grass
where your headstone rests.
Closer maybe in the stores on Cedar Lane,
a glimpse in the pharmacy window
definitely the liquor shop.

A flash of you on the stair
leading to the counselor's office.

But the glowing best of you
was there in the belly
of the firefly
flicking and flickering on Pinewood Place
as the sky turned beer-can
red and my two girls believed
finally something so small something
they could gather in their hands

could call up goose bumps

and briefly light
the dark places

the ones you know so well.

Photo by Sara Garofalo

Acknowledgements

Deepest gratitude is in order to so many who have participated in different ways on this journey. To my earliest teachers at Whittier School, who nurtured in me the love of language. To one of my first poetry teachers and the father of one of my closest childhood friends, Ted Dashman, who told me, "Your poems sound like songs." To my piano teachers, Helene Emmanuel and Edmund Neiman, who taught me lyricism, rhythm, and appreciation of sound. Profound thanks to Barbara Rockman for many wonderful writing classes, where a number of these poems were first conceived. Great respect and admiration to Kim Addonizio and Valerie Martinez, who each reviewed early versions of this book and extended deep wisdom and generous encouragement. Huge gracias to all of the devoted staff at UNM Press. Mil gracias to Hilda Raz for her impeccable guidance and wisdom and gifted editorial skills; as well as deep thanks to Elise McHugh for her unending enthusiasm and generous spirit. To my family for all of their support and their willingness to listen or reread "just one more time"; in particular my brother Tom, sister-in-law Maria, and both my daughters, Serafina and Camila, for their impeccable sense of sound. To my mother for encouraging me to keep my first journal. To Gustavo for your unfailing support, *Te amo*. To my partners in crime, my *comadres*, my sisters of the word, Catherine Ferguson, Colleen Carias, and Tina Carlson—you have always been there to listen, to nudge, to applaud, to rework. I can't imagine a world without you. To my patients, who teach me daily how to live and cope with illness in ways I might never imagine. And to Lou, who taught me so many ways to face life, not the least of which was strumming a six string and singing loud, so very loud, to the night.

Thank you to the following journals, in which some of these poems have appeared, sometimes in slightly different forms:

Adobe Walls: "You Will Find It in the Stillness"
American Journal of Nursing: "Notes to the Evening Nurse"
The Barefoot Review: "Schizophrenia"
bosque: "She Wore Opals at Her Neck," "You Left the Candle All Night," "To Reduce the Swelling," and "Spread Wide Your Arms That Might be Wings"

Connotation Press: An Online Artifact!: "Ice Candle Recipe" (published as "His Melting Face"), "Einstein on the Roof" (published as "Word Salad"), "Schizophrenia" (published as "Sing to Me") and "The Answer"
Orange Room Review: "Dipping the Dead"
Right Hand Pointing: "For Webster's Next Edition"
Redheaded Stepchild: "Here Among the Ruins"
Santa Fe Literature Review: "If Bacchus Had Left the Party Early"
Sin Fronteras: "If You Need a Wall"
Touch: A Journal of Healing: "News of a Brother's Death," "Storm Hymn" (published as "No Storm Like Him"), "Of Calamine and Honey" (winner of the 2011 Southwest Poetry Prize), "Telephone, 4 a.m.," and "You will find it in the stillness"

Thank you also to the following anthologies, in which some of these poems have appeared:

Inside Out: Literature of Mental Illness, edited by Eric Melbye and Literature for a Cause (Miami University of Ohio, 2015): "Jorge Jumped Three Times," "Time Travel," "Free Concert," "Storm Hymn," and "The Psychiatrist Said"
Silent Screams: Poetic Journeys Through Addiction and Recovery, edited by Nathaniel Granger, Jr. and Louis Hoffman (University Professors Press, 2017): "Dragon," "Delirium Tremens," "Telephone, 4 a.m."
Tzimtzum: 5 Contemporary Poets Lend Us Their Hearts (Mercury HeartLink, 2013): "Storm Hymn," "You Would Have To Be Adirondack Green Mountains," "Telephone, 4 a.m.," "Spinning with Thorazine," "The Psychiatrist Said" (published as "You Were Picturing a '68 Mustang"), "Delirium Tremens," "Arguing with Cirrhosis," "News of a Brother's Death," "Blue Vase," and "Of Calamine and Honey" (winner of the 2011 Southwest Poetry Prize)

About the Author

Katherine DiBella Seluja is a pediatric nurse practitioner and a poet. Themes of illness and healing frequently inform her writing. Recipient of the Southwest Writer's Prize for poetry, Katherine's work has appeared in the web-based 200 New Mexico Poems project, *American Journal of Nursing, bosque, Crab Orchard Review, Santa Ana River Review*, and *Touch: A Journal of Healing*, among others. Her poems "The Formula for Wholeness" and "When Your Son Is Diagnosed in the 1960s" were both nominated for a Pushcart Prize. Katherine has nursing degrees from Columbia University and Yale University. She works in pediatrics in Española, New Mexico, and as clinical faculty at the University of New Mexico in the College of Nursing. She lives in Santa Fe, New Mexico, with her husband and two daughters.